www.providencebooks.net

Publisher Contact

Email:contact@providencebooks.net

Social media: facebook.com/providencebooks

Acknowledgements

The team at Providence Books would like to thank our friends, family, suppliers and customers for making our vision of creating the highest-quality books a reality. Thanks for purchasing and enjoy the quotes!

This page is intentionally left blank

This page is intentionally left blank

'I Spy' represents the absence of the tension of the black man or black woman or anyone of that color walking in, so that the white racist person can become entertaining to a viewer.

Bill Cosby

'The Cosby Show' made an impact on comedy, television and culture. We rejected lowering the bar.

Bill Cosby

A new father quickly learns that his child invariably comes to the bathroom at precisely the times when he's in there, as if he needed company. The only way for this father to be certain of bathroom privacy is to shave at the gas station.

Bill Cosby

A word to the wise ain't necessary - it's the stupid ones that need the advice.

Bill Cosby

According to the State of Florida, the person with the gun has the right to defend him or herself.

Bill Cosby

All around the United States of America - in the cities and the counties - our public education is suffering and has been suffering. Cuts, cuts, cuts.

Bill Cosby

All parents experience the same problems.

Bill Cosby

Always end the name of your child with a vowel, so that when you yell the name will carry.

Bill Cosby

Any man today who returns from work, sinks into a chair, and calls for his pipe is a man with an appetite for danger.

Bill Cosby

As I have discovered by examining my past, I started out as a child. Coincidentally, so did my brother. My mother did not put all her eggs in one basket, so to speak: she gave me a younger brother named Russell, who taught me what was meant by 'survival of the fittest.'

Bill Cosby

Brown versus the Board of Education is no longer the white person's problem.

Bill Cosby

By the 1960s, many of us believed that the Civil Rights Movement could eliminate racism in America during our lifetime. But despite significant progress, racism remains.

Bill Cosby

Civilization had too many rules for me, so I did my best to rewrite them.

Bill Cosby

Comedy Central is what these young people are viewing. The network speaks to their audience, which is saying, 'Give me fast jokes. Give me party stories and party language.'

Bill Cosby

Decide that you want it more than you are afraid of it.

Bill Cosby

Did you ever see the customers in health - food stores? They are pale, skinny people who look half - dead. In a steak house, you see robust, ruddy people. They're dying, of course, but they look terrific.

Bill Cosby

Education happens to be something that all people, all cultures, need to embrace. Math, science, the words of the world. To be able to speak and be able to have clarity and to be able to think. Those are the greatest of gifts.

Bill Cosby

Even though your kids will consistently do the exact opposite of what you're telling them to do, you have to keep loving them just as much.

Bill Cosby

Every closed eye is not sleeping, and every open eye is not seeing.

Bill Cosby

Every success story has a parent who says, 'over my dead body.' Every success story has an old person who walks up to you and says, when you're acting the fool, 'you know I worry about you sometimes.'

Bill Cosby

Everybody is not a victim.

Bill Cosby

Family is conflict and it's something that we all relate to.

Bill Cosby

Fatherhood is pretending the present you love most is soap-on-a-rope.

Bill Cosby

For college seniors there should be a week of being allowed to cry. Just break down and cry because you are scared and don't know what's next.

Bill Cosby

George Booth and I are both funny, and from afar, without meeting, admired each other's work.

Bill Cosby

George Carlin is brilliant with words, and Johnny Winters is very creative. It's taking something common and drawing out the humor, being clever with words.

Bill Cosby

God has not made anything that I know of that pays so much attention to who their father and mother is as us.

Bill Cosby

Gray hair is God's graffiti.

Bill Cosby

Having a child is surely the most beautifully irrational act that two people in love can commit.

Bill Cosby

Human beings are the only creatures on earth that allow their children to come back home.

Bill Cosby

I am certainly not an authority on love because there are no authorities on love, just those who've had luck with it and those who haven't.

Bill Cosby

I am not going to give in to people who try to exploit me because of my celebrity status.

Bill Cosby

I am proud to be an American. Because an American can eat anything on the face of this earth as long as he has two pieces of bread.

Bill Cosby

I can't negate the theory that the Huxtables on 'The Cosby Show' may have helped pave the way for the Obama family. People enjoyed watching that black family.

Bill Cosby

I cannot understand how the education of this United States of America has been fooled time and time again. Either make it separate but equal or integrate, therefore it will be equal. And it has been separate and unequal.

Bill Cosby

I don't care what right-wing white people are thinking.

Bill Cosby

I don't have a problem believing in God and Jesus. But in Genesis one has to wonder about these sentences that just go on and end without finishing. The thought is unfinished. Where did Adam go? What is he doing? Hello? There has to be some pages missing.

Bill Cosby

I don't know the key to success, but the key to failure is trying to please everybody.

Bill Cosby

I don't see much comedy in the Bible, where people are writing about funny people. It's not there.

Bill Cosby

I don't spend my hours worrying how to slip a social message into my act.

Bill Cosby

I don't think you can bring the races together by joking about the differences between them. I'd rather talk about the similarities, about what's universal in their experiences.

Bill Cosby

I got into Temple University on a track scholarship.

Bill Cosby

I guess the real reason that my wife and I had children is the same reason that Napoleon had for invading Russia: it seemed like a good idea at the time.

Bill Cosby

I have to follow my thoughts and mine for the gold. I have to dig it out.

Bill Cosby

I love Twitter, but some people use profanity so much that at some point it's like saying, 'Pass the salt.'

Bill Cosby

I love cake. I love pie. I love potato chips. I love salt. I do not want yogurt, plain yogurt. It's healthy. 'Why don't you like it?' Because it tastes like bad breath.

Bill Cosby

I managed my life to the point that at age 19 I was still in high school. I decided I was too old to be walking down those hallways.

Bill Cosby

I never saw anything funny in a car commercial - but that's
OK. Whatever they wanted to do - it's their product and I'm the
spokesperson, and I'm going to deliver.

Bill Cosby

I often try to tell kids to think about all the people who love
you, don't cry over the one person who doesn't.

Bill Cosby

I see Obama as Sisyphus in the first four years. And nobody
would speak about the size of the rock, or the elevation of the
hill. All you hear people talk about is what he didn't do.

Bill Cosby

I tell stories. Because I believe you can do things that joke
tellers can't do, and that is, bring your audience along.

Bill Cosby

I think 'I Spy,' still when you look at it, speaks volumes in
terms of propaganda for equality. It's just magnificent.

Bill Cosby

I think I am a good running back, but I'm really not that fast. There is only one thing I can do, that is throw a cross-body block. Picture perfect. I love it. Not that good at pass blocking.

Bill Cosby

I think if a 30-year-old Bill Cosby sat on stage with a 72-year-old Bill Cosby, they would enjoy each other.

Bill Cosby

I think the part of media that romanticizes criminal behavior, things that a person will say against women, profanity, being gangster, having multiple children with multiple men and women and not wanting to is prevalent. When you look at the majority of shows on television they placate that kind of behavior.

Bill Cosby

I think you need to make responsibility something that's not just a word.

Bill Cosby

I use the exercise room early, because I don't want to get on the treadmill and everyone's going 'Oh, Bill Cosby,' and then they come around to see how fast I'm walking, and it becomes very competitive.

Bill Cosby

I want all this loud profanity in the street stopped. I want people to think about choices.

Bill Cosby

I want to get violence - I want schools to start from K through 12 to just every day have teachers understand that they don't want to talk about anything that is violent, and they want to explain to the children how bad violence is and how behavior - violent behavior, is something that they really should not practice and think about.

Bill Cosby

I was 23 years old, a freshman at university, and there I was, on the first day, sitting in a remedial English class. I was so ashamed I almost got up and left, but somehow I knew inside that if I ran away from this, I would hate myself forever.

Bill Cosby

I wasn't always black... there was this freckle, and it got bigger and bigger.

Bill Cosby

I watch an awful lot of television, and I get a little tired of what I see... We have about six television sets in our house, and it's less expensive for me to do a television series than it is for me to throw them all out.

Bill Cosby

I'm a Christian. But Muslims are misunderstood. Intentionally misunderstood. We should all be more like them.

Bill Cosby

I'm not going out and hitting a 95-mph fastball where I can't see the stitches. I'm not on a professional football team looking to tackle a fullback who is built like solid wood. I'm a thinking person, and I've been blessed with the ability to see some things and talk about them in a way that registers in a humorous and funny way.

Bill Cosby

I'm not the healthiest, but I am healthy. I'm healthy to the point where there are things that I have to eat that I don't want to eat, but I eat it because I'm enjoying staying alive.

Bill Cosby

I'm old, not dead.

Bill Cosby

I'm one of those who cut off seeing people after a certain time, when the weight is gone and they sound like the dementia is very advanced - I don't want to see that. I don't even go in to look at the body. That's not my last memory.

Bill Cosby

I've always heard about people having a conniption, but I've never seen one.

Bill Cosby

I've said all along I've never competed with 'The Simpsons.' Not in my own mind.

Bill Cosby

If I didn't like poor people, why would I come and tell them how to make their lives better?

Bill Cosby

If I read the small print, and I see that what I love to taste has pantonaponamene or fake smeinlioaimine, then I have to hide in my room when I eat it. I'm still gonna eat it, it's just gonna be 'Don't come in here!'

Bill Cosby

If the new American father feels bewildered and even defeated, let him take comfort from the fact that whatever he does in any fathering situation has a fifty percent chance of being right.

Bill Cosby

If you have no faith, you've lost your battle.

Bill Cosby

If you have one of the worst schools in the city, then chances are the teachers are not going to care for you. Chances are the parents don't feel seriously about coming to meet with teachers.

Bill Cosby

If you speak your mind and if it is true what you're saying, then I think the integrity of what you're saying carries through.

Bill Cosby

If you took your child to the dentist and check for cavities, the child likely won't get them. If you take them just for emergency, that's all they're gonna get.

Bill Cosby

If you watch kids looking at something on television, even something that's produced for them and is supposed to be funny, what you'll notice is that they don't laugh.

Bill Cosby

Immortality is a long shot, I admit. But somebody has to be first.

Bill Cosby

In September of 1960, I was blessed - and I'm not saying blessed in the everyday religious way - when Temple University accepted me after scoring 500 on the SAT. I was 23 years old, and they put me in remedial. I was the happiest remedial person on earth.

Bill Cosby

In all of my career, the style is still the same, and that is of a friend, just sitting and talking.

Bill Cosby

In order to succeed, your desire for success should be greater than your fear of failure.

Bill Cosby

It is a point of pride for the American male to keep the same size Jockey shorts for his entire life.

Bill Cosby

It isn't a matter of black is beautiful as much as it is white is not all that's beautiful.

Bill Cosby

It was hard for me, being in school. And nobody was there to tell me how important it was.

Bill Cosby

Karl Malden was a good friend of mine, and he said, 'You draw the people to you,' and I guess that's what I do.

Bill Cosby

Kids need to remember that when you put something on Twitter, it's not like whispering to your friend, you've put it on a billboard that the whole world, including your own kids someday, can see.

Bill Cosby

Laughter brings out the child in all of us.

Bill Cosby

Learning to read clusters is not something your eyes do naturally. It takes constant practice.

Bill Cosby

Let us now set forth one of the fundamental truths about marriage: the wife is in charge.

Bill Cosby

Like everyone else who makes the mistake of getting older, I begin each day with coffee and obituaries.

Bill Cosby

Men and women belong to different species and communications between them is still in its infancy.

Bill Cosby

Most of us learn to read by looking at each word in a sentence - one at a time.

Bill Cosby

My childhood should have taught me lessons for my own fatherhood, but it didn't because parenting can only be learned by people who have no children.

Bill Cosby

My feeling is, personally, I want to die first... because I believe that when you die, your soul goes immediately up for judgment - and I don't want my wife up there first. No, the judgment will be horrendous.

Bill Cosby

My observations are not bread crumbs. They do not dissolve. They are on record, on film printed in books, and found on the Internet. I am happy to share them. For this I was born.

Bill Cosby

No matter how calmly you try to referee, parenting will eventually produce bizarre behavior, and I'm not talking about the kids. Their behavior is always normal.

Bill Cosby

Nobody asked you to flip burgers for the rest of your life.

Bill Cosby

Not many jobs are available for single women who just want to have babies.

Bill Cosby

Nothing I've ever done has given me more joys and rewards than being a father to my children.

Bill Cosby

Nothing separates the generations more than music. By the time a child is eight or nine, he has developed a passion for his own music that is even stronger than his passions for procrastination and weird clothes.

Bill Cosby

Now, Richard Pryor was unique. Many misunderstood his humor. He lit up the hallway, but they didn't understand his use of profanity. He didn't use it just to be using it; he used it in the context of his satire.

Bill Cosby

Old is always fifteen years from now.

Bill Cosby

Our children are angry. The profanity is out in the street. It's on the buses and in the subway. Our children are trying to tell us something, and we are not listening.

Bill Cosby

Parents are people who yell and they yell and they yell and they yell. And you already have the point... and they're still yelling.

Bill Cosby

People can be more forgiving than you can imagine. But you have to forgive yourself. Let go of what's bitter and move on.

Bill Cosby

People have all kinds of approaches when they come up to me. Some of them are so nervous: 'You know, Mr. Cosby, you are my biggest fan!' I am? Some of them even claim that I raised them.

Bill Cosby

People say children are charming because they tell the truth. That's a lie. I've got five of them. They only tell the truth if they're in pain.

Bill Cosby

People say to me, 'Do you know who you look like?' And I say, 'I'm really tired of looking like that guy.'

Bill Cosby

Poets have said that the reason to have children is to give yourself immortality. Immortality? Now that I have five children, my only hope is that they are all out of the house before I die.

Bill Cosby

Racial humor was about 35% of my act when I first started. But I realized that it was a crutch. What brought it home was when another comedian said to me, 'If you changed color tomorrow, you wouldn't have any material.' He meant it as a put-down, but I took it as a challenge.

Bill Cosby

Raising children is an incredibly hard and risky business in which no cumulative wisdom is gained: each generation repeats the mistakes the previous one made.

Bill Cosby

Reunited with strawberry, raspberry and blueberry, I am berry, berry happy to be back working with JELL-O.

Bill Cosby

Sex education may be a good idea in the schools, but I don't believe the kids should be given homework.

Bill Cosby

Social networking helps reach people easier and quicker.

Bill Cosby

Sometimes I buy my wife flowers.

Bill Cosby

Sometimes you try to help people, and it backfires on you, and then they try to take advantage of you.

Bill Cosby

Telemarketers tell me I sound like Bill Cosby.

Bill Cosby

That married couples can live together day after day is a miracle that the Vatican has overlooked.

Bill Cosby

The absolute truth is that there is no power in celebrity.

Bill Cosby

The essence of childhood, of course, is play, which my friends and I did endlessly on streets that we reluctantly shared with traffic.

Bill Cosby

The first-born in every family is always dreaming for an imaginary older brother or sister who will look out for them.

Bill Cosby

The heart of marriage is memories; and if the two of you happen to have the same ones and can savor your reruns, then your marriage is a gift from the gods.

Bill Cosby

The main goal of the future is to stop violence. The world is addicted to it.

Bill Cosby

The most important educational vehicle in all life is a parent figure.

Bill Cosby

The past is a ghost, the future a dream, and all we ever have is now.

Bill Cosby

The problems with kids having short attention spans is driven by entertainment, reset buttons on games, games having to do with getting somewhere and heads blowing up. Everything is 'cut to the chase, cut to the chase.'

Bill Cosby

The truth is that parents are not really interested in justice. They just want quiet.

Bill Cosby

There are certain times of the day when you need a balance - that is, your protein and your carbs. I'm a Barry Sears man. I believe that anything green is a carb, and I need 2:1. Two of the carbs to one of the protein.

Bill Cosby

There are some people who have trouble recognizing a mess.

Bill Cosby

There are teachers in the United States who cry in the daytime because they see a child or children who haven't eaten properly, children who haven't used soap in so long.

Bill Cosby

There are times my stories become - what I feel - not only accessible to hearing me on television, but they make wonderful reading.

Bill Cosby

There are two sides to every story, and sometimes three, four, and five.

Bill Cosby

There is hope for the future because God has a sense of humor and we are funny to God.

Bill Cosby

There is no job a man can do that is undignified - if he does it well.

Bill Cosby

There is no labor a person does that is undignified; if they do it right.

Bill Cosby

There should be marches in every neighborhood every day telling the people about the negativity of drugs and how the drugs help us to behave negatively.

Bill Cosby

There should be more on television that uplifts people and shows them how to better prepare themselves for earning a living.

Bill Cosby

There's a gap between people knowing what I do and really believing that I still do that - and wondering what it is I really do.

Bill Cosby

There's no tradition today except initials, 'CSI,' 'NCIS,' all the rest. Even with reruns today, people don't know there was a 'Dick Van Dyke Show,' or 'Andy Griffith,' or 'Cheers.'

Bill Cosby

Things are old. Parts are old. I'm talking about 'us' parts. AARP-parts. Some of us were born with stronger parts than others.

Bill Cosby

Things from real life are the things that get people laughing.

Bill Cosby

Through humor, you can soften some of the worst blows that life delivers. And once you find laughter, no matter how painful your situation might be, you can survive it.

Bill Cosby

Tons of comedians have said, 'I grew up learning from Bill Cosby. He's great.' But that respect doesn't mean much to the young people. They like their ginger ale with hot sauce.

Bill Cosby

Too many people are waiting for Jesus to come along and cut your grass. And Jesus isn't going to come along and cut your grass.

Bill Cosby

We are all anxious to be accepted. But if you have a strong mother and father who tell you that you don't have to dress a crazy way, or hang out with people who are looking for trouble in order to be loved and accepted, then half the battle is over.

Bill Cosby

We're not raising children with the love that we need to.

Bill Cosby

We've got to get the gun out of the hands of people who are supposed to be on neighborhood watch.

Bill Cosby

We've got too many young girls, who don't know how to parent, turning themselves into parents.

Bill Cosby

What kept me out of trouble is going right to the edge and then... thinking that my mother would be embarrassed, and that I didn't want to embarrass her, and that my father would be embarrassed, and I just didn't want to do that to my family.

Bill Cosby

What people are tired of, the people who agree with me, what they're tired of is listening to that sound, the sound of the people who've given up.

Bill Cosby

What we need is for people to realize - 'I want to raise my kid. I want to go back and get my three kids. I want to take on that responsibility. I want to love my children.'

Bill Cosby

When Bob Dylan was a beginning fellow, Len Chandler, a black singer-musician who played a 12-string guitar, was a friend of his.

Bill Cosby

When I decided that I wanted to go to college, I wanted to be a school teacher for 7th and 8th grade boys because I felt that was an important time for them. I had gone astray at that point in my life and really wanted to help keep them from making the same mistake I had made.

Bill Cosby

When I look at 55 percent of our black men dropping out of school, how bad off are we going to be when we need some lawyers?

Bill Cosby

When I say, I don't care what white people think, I mean that.

Bill Cosby

When I was a boy if a girl got pregnant the shame was placed on her and the boy could get away.

Bill Cosby

When I was a child, I was living in the housing projects of Philadelphia. I didn't even have a Christmas tree.

Bill Cosby

When a person has a gun, sometimes their mind clicks that this thing will win arguments and straighten people out.

Bill Cosby

When my son was murdered, people asked me how I felt about God and what had happened to my son. I said, 'No, you can't go there. You have to understand that there is a devil, and he works 24/7. Whoever murdered our son was with the devil.'

Bill Cosby

When you become senile, you won't know it.

Bill Cosby

When you carry a gun, you mean to harm somebody, kill somebody.

Bill Cosby

When you don't understand something, you often laugh.

Bill Cosby

When you introduce competition into the public school system, most studies show that schools start to do better when they are competing for students.

Bill Cosby

With my wife Camille's help, I took to social networking. I'm working with the computers.

Bill Cosby

Women don't want to hear what you think. Women want to hear what they think - in a deeper voice.

Bill Cosby

You can turn painful situations around through laughter. If you can find humor in anything, even poverty, you can survive it.

Bill Cosby

You can't compete with Walmart. But you can have smaller businesses that are successful.

Bill Cosby

You can't prove somebody is a racist unless they really come out and do the act and is found to be that.

Bill Cosby

You come to my comedy show to be entertained.

Bill Cosby

You don't know what you're going to fall in love with until you're exposed to it.

Bill Cosby

You don't reinvent yourself; you get better with what you do.

Bill Cosby

You know the only people who are always sure about the proper way to raise children? Those who've never had any.

Bill Cosby

This page is intentionally left blank

This page is intentionally left blank

This page is intentionally left blank

This page is intentionally left blank

This page is intentionally left blank